# The Heart is a House

# The Heart is a House

*The Selected Poems of Emily J. Cooper*

Published 2019

Copyright © 2019 by Emily Joan Cooper

All rights reserved. No part of this publication may be reproduced, distributed, or transmitted in any form or by any means without the prior written permission of the publisher, except in the case of brief quotations embodied in critical reviews and certain other noncommercial uses permitted by copyright law.

First Printing: 2019

ISBN 978-0-578-47373-4

Publisher:
Emily Joan Cooper
Peabody, Massachusetts

U.S. trade bookstores and wholesalers: Please contact Emily Cooper at
emilyjoancooper@gmail.com

The Font Type is "IM FELL English."
The Fell Types are digitally reproduced by Igino Marini.
www.iginomarini.com

Book cover designed and illustrated by Emily Cooper

Published and printed in the United States of America

*Dedicated to Evan who taught me to churn steadily through itty-bitty pockets of time in order to take a dream and give it legs to stand on.*

# Table of Contents

Author's Note......................................................................... xi

## It's in Our Nature

Often I am Dreaming................................................................ 15
Windblown Light..................................................................... 16
Breath...................................................................................... 17
Springtime in Davis Square ................................................... 18
Ice............................................................................................ 19
First Sights.............................................................................. 20
Wording .................................................................................. 21
Garden Dream........................................................................ 22
Hopping Over Garden Walls ................................................. 24
Cloud ...................................................................................... 25
On Guard................................................................................ 26
Symphonies and Silence......................................................... 27
Autumnal ................................................................................ 28
The Fly ................................................................................... 29
The Egret ............................................................................... 30
Reveries................................................................................... 31
Often He is Dreaming............................................................ 32

## Maine

Wake-Up Call......................................................................... 35
Behind You............................................................................. 36
J.L.C....................................................................................... 37
He's Not That Into You ........................................................ 39
For a Friend............................................................................ 40
Mt. Desert Island ................................................................... 41

Return from Vacation .................................................... 42

## Traveler

Somewhere a Train ...................................................... 45
Alluvia ........................................................................ 46
Refugees ...................................................................... 47
A Thought ................................................................... 48
We Are Conveyed ....................................................... 49

## Psyche

Synapses ...................................................................... 53
On Burning Bridges .................................................... 54
Bones ........................................................................... 55
Shock and Stifle .......................................................... 56
Losing Pieces ............................................................... 57
Dislocation .................................................................. 58
Intravenous ................................................................. 59
But Then it Aches ....................................................... 60
When ........................................................................... 61
Weekdays, 8:45 AM .................................................... 62
Directions .................................................................... 63

## Fables

Down by the Water ..................................................... 67
Star Fishing ................................................................. 68
Fear Names .................................................................. 70
Sea Stone ..................................................................... 71
Phantom Hollow ......................................................... 72
Limbo .......................................................................... 73
Gravestones ................................................................. 74

My Friend David ............................................................... 75
The Owl ............................................................................ 76
The Raven ........................................................................ 77

## Architectures

Gazing at the Chapel .......................................................... 81
Steel ................................................................................. 82
Mimes ............................................................................... 83
The Worship Game ............................................................ 84
New Boston ...................................................................... 85
Looking Through Windows ................................................ 86

## Traces of Home

Christmas Eve ................................................................... 89
July ................................................................................... 90
The Fourth of July ............................................................. 91
Summer Storm .................................................................. 92
Thanksgiving Firsts ........................................................... 93
The Snow Makes Me Think of Death ................................. 94
Homesick .......................................................................... 97
Threads ............................................................................ 98
Beasts of Wilmette ............................................................ 99
War ................................................................................ 100
On Leaving My House for the Last Time .......................... 101
Shrapnel ......................................................................... 103
Goodbye House .............................................................. 104
New Rooms .................................................................... 105
Scars .............................................................................. 106
A Different State ............................................................. 107
Reflection ....................................................................... 108
The Architecture of Memory ............................................ 109

Who Are You, House?........................................................... 110

## *You I Have Loved*

A Ghost I Knew................................................................ 113
The Heart is a House......................................................... 114
Daybreak...................................................................... 115
Passersby..................................................................... 116
Joya.......................................................................... 118
Her Hands (By NTS)............................................................ 119
Corta Pero Ancha.............................................................. 120
Mainly in the World........................................................... 122
Benediction................................................................... 123
It Helps, a Little............................................................ 124
How to Turn on a Lamp......................................................... 125
King Biko..................................................................... 126
Pocket-concert................................................................ 128
Homecomings (By JPS).......................................................... 129
Love Them Well................................................................ 130
In Here....................................................................... 131
Home is the Heart............................................................. 132

# Author's Note

❀

I'm not well studied in poetry as a craft—I merely enjoy reading it and indulging the impulse to write. So, what gives me the right to publish a book of poetry without understanding it better? I've asked myself this question a hundred times. I can only say that writing over the course of these many years has been a joy, a therapy, and a necessity. Although there are many authors more educated, talented, and prolific than I, I must believe this is reason enough.

I began writing in 2000 or 2001 after a man who called himself "The Poetry Man" waltzed into my 7th-grade classroom with sheaves of poetry in a backpack and a king's share of passion for it. He opened my eyes to a world of artistry through words and in retrospect he did look like a young Bob Ross. Unfortunately, my writing from those early days is lost or buried in cardboard boxes somewhere in the Midwest. Probably for the best—back then I wrote exclusively as a poor exercise in rhyming. At any rate, once I started writing I never stopped and thankfully I believe my style has morphed into something more organic.

Regarding this book, it was deliciously challenging to edit something I've been so close to for so long. Through the process, I often referred to a copy of *Roget's Thesaurus*—the last gift my grandfather gave me before he passed away in December of 2017. He was my kindred spirit in many ways, including our mutual love of language. With *Roget* in my hands, I felt I was still communing with him, in a sense. Furthermore, as I began compiling and rereading my work, I came to realize that many of the initial wordings I used were based on love of particular words or the impact of their sounds over genuine communication. I knew that wasn't going to be good enough.

My goal became honesty above all things. I had to break free of old patterns. Armed with *Roget* I took pen to paper time and time again, molding each poem into what I felt it was trying to say at its core. I know this may sound hyperbolic, but in all seriousness, giving these poems materiality through this little book has been a way to give my life a greater sense of meaning. It has been a way to plant a flag in the soil, so-to-speak, and say what we have needed to say since the dawn of our time: "I was here."

As the world is both a dark and beautiful place, to interpret it through an art form of any kind makes it more bearable and lends it more magic. I know I'm not alone in saying this is something I dearly need. I can promise you a few things as you read on: you will find something simple, pretentious, unusual, cliché, whimsical, painful, and hopeful. You will find something you relate to, something you enjoy, and likely something you don't. You'll even find guest appearances from my poetic family. Ultimately, you honor me by reading this book that is such a huge and vulnerable part of me, and for that I am deeply grateful.

Without further ado, here are the fruits of my poetic labor between childhood and adulthood (though forgive me—I did exclude a few poems from my teen years that were a little *too* self-indulgent). Now let's toast to cherished books and treasured words, to the beautiful with the macabre, the magic within the ordinary, the weird with the wonderful—all which make up our human experience. Here's to all we've lost, all we have, and all we have yet to gain from this life. Here's to you, lovely thing.

P.S. Please laugh with me now at *The Fly*. I was young and despite the melodrama, there was no irony intended. Can you stand it? I was being completely serious.

*It's in Our Nature*

# Often I am Dreaming

Often I am dreaming
of the provenance of thrushes;
the river's domain,
the oaken kingdom.

I imagine that Wood
in the misty blue hour—
drops of light twinkling
from each singing tree.

Often I am dreaming
of quietude's homestead,
the twitch of a hare's ear,
cool brooks over stones.

Always a breeze,
a snail in the mud,
the last strains of night,
trout dances.

# Windblown Light

There's a windblown light
Coming in through my window
And the sound of the birds
Makes it seem so absurd
That there ever was strain in my heart.

# Breath

The things I've seen
fly wingless—
flecks of snow or spots of ash,
bright pink petals or russet leaves—
are to me the very proof
the world is breathing
in and
out.

## Springtime in Davis Square

The petals fall,
    silent, pale like
        snow.
Casting shadows in the gutters they form
    mounds scented like sugar
        and decay.
Propelled by passing wheels they tumble.
    Blowing over sidewalks
        they fly off into the endless blue,
        and on and so on.

# Ice

A dollop of sun, pink
spill on window frost,
sinks and disappears
like clinquant scales
beneath the sea—
half-remembered
glints in all
this silence. I
wait for the birds
to return.

# First Sights

Thin elastic cloud—
a dull, gray morning light
filling the room.

A pale curtain,
a metal desk,
a wooden dresser,
a pink phone

touched by it.

# Wording

I don't know what lilac smells like.
If I saw juniper or foxglove
I couldn't name them.
I've no idea what hyssop is
or what color graces lady slipper, but
I do know the arched reflection of the window
on the closet's porcelain doorknob
in the morning.
I know the wording
on the underside
of the coffee table,
and the shade of blue
on our bedroom walls: "Opal Silk."
I can conjure with my mind
the musty aroma of the basement,
or the Blue Jays' raucous reports
over the mellow strains of WCRB.
I have house slippers the color of a rose.
These are baluster and balustrade.
The hand soap smells like lemongrass,
so they say.

## Garden Dream

I had a dream the other night
about a garden old and wild,
in it stood a tower of stone
flanked with roses lushly piled.

The scent was potent, rare and fierce—
so strong it made you wish for sleep,
to settle in the whisper grass
and roll the soil over your feet.

I wandered in the golden hour,
collecting blooms and chasing light,
when all at once my blood ran cold
and all within me pulsed with fright.

There was no need to look behind—
I sensed an evil rising there—
panting, sprinting, scraping, huffing
desperately to maim and tear.

I flew headlong into the garden,
tripped into a hidden pool
and sinking to its murky bottom,
met a thing even more cruel:

eyes of mirth and rows of teeth—
perversions I cannot convey—
I could not think, I could not breathe,
there was no time to get away.

High overhead the canopy
was billowing in shades of green
and not a soul alive beneath
would ever speak of what they'd seen.

A blackbird perched upon my body,
pecking, tearing at my shoulder—
in my pain I cried and wakened
soaked in blood and ten years older.

# Hopping Over Garden Walls

Hopping over garden walls
I often feel the thorns—
digging into sole and skin
while I go seeking sweetness.

Amber, lilac, fuchsia, gold,
bright and sweet and merry—
all the flowers of this spring
come painfully, I tarry.

# Cloud

Let me hold onto
this glinting revelation—
angelic, yes!
How close I am to home!
For a moment I'm above
a face,
above
a name,
above
myself.
This moment I'm
suspended
high on high,
sheer and bursting,
full of light!
Oh let us all be clouds.

## On Guard

The shadows lie long and thick
in the parlor. A woman
lifts a hand, unfurls her fingers
and reveals a palm as soft as
a magnolia petal.
She rests her chin upon it.

The hour sounds from the great clock
on guard over the hall. Somewhere
behind thick curtains, a fly traverses a field of panes—
its wings ringing like machine guns.
A vase crashes in the foyer.
Twilight falls.

## Symphonies and Silence

Heavenly pools manifest across the marshes—
patios of gilded sky bearing cranes and egrets.
Insects droning in the high heat lie hidden
by sweet grasses and floral lace,
igniting hums within my ribcage
thrumming which each crescendo and
decrescendo—*con allegria, legato.*

Beyond, the glassy sea repines—
delighting in the sun's descent.
Borrowing her winsome gleam,
its grandeur dampens every chord.
Here, on a terrace of lichen and stone,
there is only beholding,
there is only silence.

## Autumnal

Doesn't it feel like the walls of the world
close in more tightly in the Autumn?
As though in twilight, porch lights go on shining but
from somewhere tucked a little farther
in the thickened gloaming.

Feel it riding up your spine,
leaves blowing down an alleyway,
rustling and crinkling in the chill—
a strange sensory simulacrum—
a whisper, a breeze on the nape.

Once low and tame,
the harbor is full to the brim—
deeper and darker, foamed at the lips,
singing a song
that coddles.

On the other side of the bay a beacon
lays down an orange cape, wavering
on the cold surface. The sky,
heavy with steel wool, rolls and rolls
away, scraping steeples.

# The Fly

The fly between the windowpanes
Upon the windowsill
Gazed out upon a snow-cold world—
Both him and this were still.

His last thoughts trapped within this tomb,
Last moment still portrayed—
The fly looked toward an endless world
From which he was delayed.

The swaying pines, the flowing wind,
To whisper ever clear
And tempt him of this freedom
Of which he was so near.

The brown bird sings, the morning dawns,
On what day, who knows which?
Yet here so far and yet so close,
His wings a final twitch.

# The Egret

I watched an egret soar
over the waters of the Charles.
Mesmerized, I remembered
what it felt like to be clean.

Beyond the streaked windows of the train
the morning sky was gray as a moth's wing,
a dense fog settling over the city
like a tattered shawl.

All was dripping with the ashen dew
of a baffled December but the egret—
pale, slender, slow—was gliding
low across the river like a gloved hand.

# Reveries

Hummingbird mind
flits over memory—
*the islands were
enveloped in fog this morning,
that hollow tree looked
like a little house,
there is no mountain laurel in this town
(toxic, blushing
little stars).*
Bleak parallels emerge
from wan mists
and dark woods.

# Often He is Dreaming

Often he is dreaming
of the provenance of horses;
the eagle's domain,
the sage kingdom.

I imagine his world
at the crepuscule hour—
serried backs of mountains drawing fire
and blistering starlight from the sky.

*Maine*

## Wake-Up Call

With the fan pondering east and west
and a bare leg buried under a mountain of down,
I keep my eyes half-open, clinging onto sleep,
warming to the sun—

it's white-gold
and shouting,
"Love!"
Again.

With a stretch
I emerge from a cocoon
of crumpled sheets
and latent dreams.

Two feet touch down on a worn rug,
a puff of dust dazzles
in the air.
Footsteps echo in the stairwell.

Alert,
I race tiptoe to the foyer,
pulling down a nest of hair I gnaw lips
pale from hibernating.

Breathless,
an ear pressed to the door,
the pounding sounds
inside me.

The neighbors greet a friend
and I welcome your absence,
sit us down, and serve us both
a steaming cup of coffee.

## Behind You

The photograph of us
could not have better told
the story of you and me.
There you stand,
handsome,
looking forward,
eyes fixed
on all that lies
ahead.
Small,
I walk up behind you,
eyes down on the rocks.
Though I wobble
on those stones
I look stable.
I look ready
to embrace you from behind
and love you blindly.

# J.L.C.

Waiting for the light
at the broad intersection
we are struck by the brilliance of red.
Fall has never been so colorless
but here, beside the cemetery,
a clot of trees
with leaves like outstretched fingers
snatches the light and glows.

We drive on
and park the car beside
the Goodwill where
I hear a woman with hair like
singed cinnamon say,
"I used to be a nun,"
while shifting through bleached,
secondhand lingerie.

As we exit she stands beside a cart.
Her eyes alight on anything
but the massive heap—
a crucifix for sale
of every shape and size.
Wood, metal, clay—
a roadside Jesus
for every living room.

Nearing home we slow to see
the face of a bronze hero
mocked by a white medical mask.
High on his pedestal he does not succumb,
though we know the strength of an epidemic.
Joshua Lawrence Chamberlain—
infected

like all the rest.

On we go,
on he stares.
So sure of our resplendent
denim-blue sky,
a soldier points
to those beneath the tree line
who'll never know that a red sunset
scintillates on the horizon.

## He's Not That Into You

The urgency of night knows
nothing of real need, only perfumed skin—
the inner elbow.
Shucking shoes like children
shelling mothers,
shedding fathers,
stripping brothers and sisters and
aunts with narrow-hips-big-smiles
bestowed on higher bidders,
coming undone.

Bedlocked, shielding flesh from
the frozen breath of the world with
blankets pulled overhead, to fortress,
a January frost glimmers outside.
Reclasping and reclaiming
(what?), hastily
dropping silences that
settle like disappointments
between the floorboards, in the empty shoes,
under the bed, with the dust.

Notice how,
sweet one,
the lamplight outside is more old-tooth-yellow
than remembered.
The sun is rising.

Get home and flex toes in the predawn
as memory wisps over a body—
a palm, a lash—
and is gone.

## For a Friend

We ride into the night across a river of asphalt and dust.
In the lot, light melts over scrappy patches of grass,
bottle caps, and long forsaken clotheslines.

Apartment windows making an imperfect,
toothy smile, grin
knowingly as we pass.

Two bikes—idle by the stoop—
stand lip-locked and propped, perhaps, in prayer
for love or answers.

If the universe lay in that river of darkness beyond the curb
like I suggested and you imagined (all stars and spinning
neon galaxies), would you leap? Would I?

## Mt. Desert Island

A loose lampshade sways like a church bell
or tightly garbed hips in the cold breath
of an oscillating fan.
I tied a palm-sized kite to those dusty grates
caging petals of blades,
rolling like the wheel of a mill with a vengeance.

Small blue kite—
enforced but
willing psychopath—
caught in relentless turbulence
with its tail
trailing behind.

I won't bring up
how you placed me on the shelf
like another faded shell
or bit of jetsam
when *she*
came back.

You might escape (deny)
those words that formed on our tongues
all those times we talked by the cliffside
and listened and watched for some sign—
out here I learn
each woman is an island.

## Return from Vacation

The air so still
I thought I could feel the lilies
reaching for the light.
Poor things were left behind,
the room in
constant night.

The humming fridge a
cold, chrome,
cavernous heart.
The rain begins to pour
and wash the cars out front.

*Traveler*

## Somewhere a Train

The judgment of the wind
over the wheat proclaimed,
"No more silence"
and swept upon the stalks.

Brushing shyly,
neither felt the touch.
Grains whispered, bodies
swayed, swooned, shushed.

Somewhere a train
trails a bloom of mournful blue—
an acrid stain pours out over
the countryside.

No one sees or hears
the golden field whipping,
the scream
of the train,

the sky resounding,
shaking the soil.
The world had been too still,
thus judged the bitter southbound wind.

# Alluvia

Red desert sands surround green scrub across the valley—
the backs of beasts long gone bake in a merciless sun,
gathering rogue brambles. All the day is red
until extinguished in this world's only offering
of ultramarine. The burnt clouds bow at last and sizzle out.

In town a few palms rustle dryly
above beige gravel, khaki stucco, and tan stones.
The mountains beyond sing
an ancient hymn to the sky—
pinched earth entreating, *"Lluvia. Por favor..."*

The raised highway transecting the valley
paves a way for brittle Ford pickups. Without warning
the vacancy overhead cracks open. Instantly, all is subaquatic.
There is no choice but to stop and wait while the road is sluiced,
leaving alluvia.

# Refugees

The years collect on once gleaming surfaces—
young beatific spirits sinking
day by day under skins slickly spattered by
their struggles, and by time.

Cast from hometowns, homelands, house shoes,
hopeful, and afraid
they set out on their pilgrimage—
the mountains grow an inch.

Between the valley walls in mottled shadow, limestone, and dust,
their wake is marked by crooked grins each facing in
toward one another—all alike, soon,
all forgot.

They go and claw against the crags,
dreaming of ascent.
The further on they stumble the further they erode,
Meanwhile the wind-carved tunnels howl, "Return..."

They march until they stand in sea foam, chins on the horizon.
Barnacles appear like stars on earth-stained legs and
lips parted, they call out.
Thousands—watching the divide until it ceases to exist.

The canyons far behind are crumbling.
The forests—rattling like a province of dry bones.
Wading on, they fall into the lap of the landscape
and are rocked.

# A Thought

The propellers of a Saab 340b
shock the rain into a hazy spray
and the buzzing of potential starts.
A phrase from thin air disturbs my mind:
"The art of losing
isn't hard to master."

An omen, I wonder?
Will I be punished for the thought
and in a burning heap of metal and flame
fall from the heavens
and so easily
lose everything?

If given the option
to be lost
or someday—
in form or formlessness—
be found again,
I choose obliteration.

# We Are Conveyed

"All rise" a voice commands.
Eyes forward we oblige,
raise our hands over our heads
and pull short histories down
from plastic cabinets.

Beyond an oval window I observe
a caravan of packages followed
by a train of fifty boxed azalea plants
gliding like an improbable dream into rough hands,
and being shucked into the cold indigo trolley.

A wealth of magenta proudly glances out,
parading light beneath the city toxins.
Tender cargo, an arrow on each side points
to the gray arch of the sky.

I wonder in the sounding
of my heart with sudden fright,
is anything so lovely
as azaleas in flight?

*Psyche*

## Synapses

In me, moving, wired, untamed,
   Gnawing, quiet, silent, lame,
Gray and blackened, pouring, drained,
   Listing, listing all your names.

Grown and growing bigger now—
   The worm that feeds upon the boughs
Where love as leaves falls to the ground
   And building there they have no out.

No gardener here to tame the buds,
   To trim the hedges of that love.
No decomposing though I wish—
   For then the new, the old begets,

And with such growth
   The past forget,
But lists and branches
   Catch my breath.

## On Burning Bridges

Sometimes you think you've burned a bridge
   You turned away and tossed the match
But one day when you're walking by
   You see the fire didn't catch.

# Bones

Like a hooped skirt
like a trellis
like the arched ribs
of a greenhouse.
Like the air in a balloon,
and the water in a glass,
and the meat in the fridge.

These bones become a building.
This skin becomes a roof.
Something mute and divine
asks me to observe
what we are,
*how* we are.
What weird,
fucked-up little beings.

## Shock and Stifle

You can button up
from sternum to throat,
make your mouth a tight, fine line
and will your heart to silence
rather than tell your story.

Soft eyes and placid brow
are one way to deal with a blow.
You might remain as smooth and clear
and cold as a high winter's sky
or a sparkling virgin snowfield.

Thoughts and feelings might be
scattered like red berries across the floe,
shot up like clover over a frostbitten lawn, or
spilled like dark beads over the frozen drifts—
but these one can gather up,

mow down,
bury.
You might even tie them up in dark velvet
and wear them on your hip like a prize,
remarking, "This old thing? It's nothing."

## Losing Pieces

She lost her diamond ring—
left it on a speckled countertop
in a hospital bathroom,
came back for it later and found nothing
but an incandescent bubble on the sink ledge in its place.

I, too, am that woman
losing her jewels, losing her pieces and
letting them drop to the ground
(sometimes deliberately)
over the path behind.

Looking for them
from time to time,
thinking they'll appear
in the hands of a stranger.
Counting on it.

## Dislocation

I thought I'd lost
my self—
that bit inside
where words grow wings
of lunar moths

and colors pour like milk from mouths;
where ice melts up and sunlight smells like jasmine
and trees grow arms and legs and roam.
Not lost, dislocated. You grasped me
tight, whispered my name and set me right.

I learn we will forever be
ridding ourselves of this,
and that, losing and
shedding and metamorphosing
like changelings, together.

# Intravenous

Inside is hot and roiling—
a pot ready to drain
and scald.

Inside is frozen pain—
burning arctic tundra
to be carved out like ice cream.

A black seed,
an ink stain in the water,
such a slow, bright tide.

It's not a splinter in the thumb,
it's something in the blood.

## But Then it Aches

Sometimes you're glad to see
a bit of your own blood—
river of life
moving in you—
to know you're not alone.

Like a king tide,
not unbeautiful, this grief is
languid and liquiform—
out of body,
wave after wave over your head.

Soon cradled memory from the heart
of a tangible wound will surface.
Ebbing, flowing, leaving
dark pools and scattered voids—
everywhere stinging, everything sparkling.

At the core of it—
a peace.
Such silence,
a conceding to something sublime—
a known truth.

One I loved has gone
to the unknowable expanse.
I have no more salt to bathe in
and no healing swells in me now—
just a copper, arid desert.

I am composed but oh,
I can ache.

# When

When stars reappear for me
and the catch in my chest transmutes to keening.

When the skies refill with blood orange horizons,
violet in cumulous, and sapphire at the day's goodbye.

When I wake and hear bells,
and the hate in my hands burns out.

When I've stopped gnashing my teeth
and there's nothing left to ruin, only then

will I paint again.
No force could bring me to it now.

## Weekdays, 8:45 AM

Slow intestinal burns and
cardiac microsplosions.
It's time to pack up the sparkling things,
the confetti,
the pastel clouds,
the tiny stars,
the monsters and the little darlings.
It's time to go to work.

# Directions

Moored boats point in the direction of the wind.
One great lone sunflower points in the direction of the boats.
An old man in a red coat spins, pointing no direction at all.
I watch him in my rear-view mirror growing smaller,
and drive in the direction of the wind.

*Fables*

# Down by the Water

Down by the water
   are two sequin skies.
The frozen dock screams,
   the winter wind sighs.

The icy bay whispers
   rock into the deep
with the tall grass resisting
   the push of my feet.

I'm running for fear
   of this thing in my dream
and the faster I run
   the slower the speed.

There's something that's coming
   from up underneath—
the water is rising,
   so cold it's like heat.

Down by the water,
   down in the water,
down on the water
   the winter wind sighs.

## Star Fishing

At night I bring my fishing pole into the open plain,
   All set in cap and trousers marching down the dirt path main.
Upon my hand my finger wore a starry ring of silver,
   Shapes of constellations that within the moonlight quiver.

I tie my hair back in a bow and see the cratered jewel,
   And let my gaze roam upward to the boundless navy pool.
Arriving in the center of the endless grassy wave,
   I finished the ham sandwich that my dear old mother gave.

My tackle box is set upon a rock below a tree,
   And here I bait the sharp hook I would soon let fly and free.
The breeze rustled the leaves above, the quiet was immense,
   The crickets made the noise of life, resounding so intense.

Concentrating in this light, I cast out the line,
   Into the tranquil current spinning 'bove the mighty pine.
And in this sky I truly saw the twinkling of small eyes,
   Winking and a-blinking as a candle from a sigh.

Here and now I rest among the swaying reeds and flowers,
   Nodding off in wait through the eternal nightly hours...
Suddenly I feel a tug between my waiting hands,
   A victim of the starry sea is fooled by my plans!

I jump up to my feet and stand there planted in the field,
   The shooting blur of light fights as I take hold of the reel!
I pull! It soars! I close the space between myself and he—
   The laughing, daunting prince of night who then called out to me:

"Let me go o dear one who walks there upon the earth,
   Do you not see that I'm not meant to walk upon the turf?
I dwell among the silver and the gold of the night sky,
   Whose beauty would be lost if brought to where no star can lie.

Quickly I would fade, becoming dull and without shine,
   I'd be just another human, 'stead of something quite divine.

Release me now and I will swear to guide you every night,
   And always be above you as a clear and constant light."

Upon his words I pondered and decided it was right,
   To let my fellow shining friend into the dark of night.
I reeled him in quite close so I could then remove the hook,
   And saw within his face the handsome shimmer of his look.

Would I now capture him within my arms and hold him here?
   Only to keep him human, he would wither with each year.
I felt a pain within my heart as I then let him go,
   But before he dashed away I ought to let you know…

He left me with a gift when he saw that my heart was weak—
   He gave to me a gleaming kiss upon my rosy cheek.
It soaked into my skin and pulsed and flowed within my veins,
   Some swear they see a light aglow behind my eyes these days.

"Goodbye, dear friend!" I called into the glowing morning haze,
   And so I packed my things up and resolved my fishing days.
Now each night he shares with me the light with which he's blessed,
   For beauty's better off alive than picked to dull with all the rest.

## Fear Names

Name your fear something like "Henry,"
   I've a "Richard" and a "Fred."
Say a prayer for all of them
   Each night before you go to bed.

Tuck them in and whisper, "Darling,
   You've got sense to walk with me."
Hold them close and comfort them,
   For they are nothing without thee.

# Sea Stone

The smooth, sunbaked stone radiated heat in my closed fist.
I rinsed it in the cool tide of the Pacific.
With its dry skin bathed and cooled
it glimmered with the specks of a sea-king's throne,
so I put it back.

## Phantom Hollow

A man with a heart full of spiders and sorrow,
   Cobwebs and darkness, dreams and despair,
Watched over a lady as silken as satin,
   As frail as a swallow, as wild as her hair.

Brittle as sugar she fell from the stairwell
   And like an old tree she grew into her chair—
Just as the branches grow thick round the fences
   And prisons that hold them, they'll reach for the air.

All the bright children with gumption and courage
   Knock loudly so sounding an echoing din.
The walls and the hallways resound with the pounding
   So harshly surrounding the elders within.

Deliberate and slow as a saltwater tide,
   The man full of spiders attends the front door—
The hollow behind him will scarcely define him
   "Colossal the mansion of death!" they'll report.

The children flee weeping to find a warm mother
   And tell all their brothers the horror they'd seen:
A lady in white who'd grown into a chair
   And a man with an outline and nothing between.

# Limbo

At the root of all things is a heart
   And the buds of the heart ever thrive;
Although beaten and wracked by the snow,
   They do what they must—they survive.

A circlet of goldenrod branches—
   Of earth and yet somehow divine—
Encircles the flesh of this heart
   In a world made of perfect design.

Is it soil, is it air, is it man
   That engenders the love of a God
Who would carry you next to his bosom
   And then lay you down soft on the sod?

How the pain of his love pierces through me—
   In my palms and my soles and my veins—
While he bathes me in honey and milk,
   At the rose-tender sound of a name.

Keep me no longer in limbo,
   Return me to earth or to sky,
Because holding me here in the heart of these things
   Means that surely, soon, I would die.

# Gravestones

Upon the pretty flower beds
   Fall proverbs that the prophets said,
Which plant themselves like graves and read,
   "We fear not death but dying."

And all the pretty ladies knew
   That no amount of rouge could do
The likes of what the youthful knew
   The handsome lads were eyeing.

If only all the aged could see—
   The fruitless fight: Authority!
And in its stead let Artwork be,
   Then could the soul go flying.

Now all the clocks in all the shops
   And all the cuckoos tarry not
Reminding all we are begot
   To time we bank on buying.

Oh spenders, they are lying!
   No salesman sells what you are trying blindly to conceive—
A frothy, pretty dream. There never was such thing
   As everlasting kings.

# My Friend David

I found it on the windowsill,
   Waiting just for me—
A speckled bit of spectral cloth
   Just like the prophecy.

I picked it up, held it aloft,
   All fell into a hush.
Then whispered in my ear a voice—
   "Away, away at once!"

I felt afeared but did not go
   I took the cloth and ate it,
And saw at once in front of me,
   A little boy named David.

Hand in hand we walked until
   We found his little grave.
The years had turned the stone to dust
   But still this was the place.

He thanked me and he kissed my hand
   And stepped into the mound.
No sooner did he sleep that I awoke here
   With a frown...

In my own home, in my own bed,
   Corporeal once more,
And there upon the sill a crown
   Of posies from the moor.

# The Owl

Once upon a time there was a girl with crimson curls,
    Her heart was full of rosemary and rye.
She was sitting on a sandbank when a wild wind unfurled,
    The birds in all the trees began to cry.

Oh the storm is coming and will ruin her white gown!
    Oh the earth will want her there to rest!
She stood holding a flower as the sea crept all around,
    And crying out she clutched it to her chest.

"Let mother well remember me and also father dear!"
    She let the petals catch the wind and fly.
No sooner had she let go that a great white owl appeared
    And caught a yellow petal in the sky.

The sea was rising high now as she flailed and watched the owl,
    Who stole the petal high into the clouds.
At once he disappeared and soon the heathen weather cowered—
    The veil of gray became a golden shroud.

The girl with hair of ebony was whisked unto the shore,
    She turned and went on skipping home to town.
A thousand silver puddles shone from east point unto west,
    Within one lay a feather white as down.

# The Raven

There lived a woman in a tower
   Made of shining ivory stone.
Though no words would break her stillness,
   There she did not dwell alone—

Perched upon an oaken wardrobe
   Was a bird of ebon black.
He knew all the worldly blunders
   And the good that people lacked.

So he stayed and was her keeper
   'Til the day she left to roam—
Put aside his dire warnings
   To explore the great unknown.

She returned in fifty years
   Bent and tired, sad and poor,
But instead of her old friend
   Found just his feathers on the floor.

*Architectures*

# Gazing at the Chapel

Tonight tight constellations
spin out high over the steeples.
A chapel dozes
while its windows let seep
a pool of gold.
One stained glass wheel glows
in the back.

These rows and
throws of light
lie so unassumingly
en masse.
It appears the panes
are made of tracing paper,
the bricks are painted foam.

# Steel

Landscapes of steel
took down our red bricks;
those gardens
of sun-soaked begonia and glass.
They chipped all the mortar
into the dark waters
where residue builds
lichen cities,
halls of stone.

# Mimes

Concrete sprouts
in heavy stems still rising
toward the sun—
earnest tendrils reaching
for the heights.

Dwarfed I stand
in bitter grasses
sprouting sparse between,
where I can only pantomime
their gesture for a dream.

# The Worship Game

Lacing fingers together en revés,
pointer fingers rising to say, "Here is the steeple."
Unfolding palms reveal ondas de dedos,
waves of worshipping worms,
toda la gente, right there,
waiting for a witness.

# New Boston

A nickel pressed in
concrete. Money city, built on
money. Fractured and frigid and
smoke filled
I feel like a child
in its shadow—
so dim you could dry up and
whither in it,
another crumple
in the gutter.

Sewer grates,
a cigarette stub, no,
five.
A crosswalk.
A pair of slacks.
A sky
cracking open overhead.
Light, smooth steel and gray
glass, shining.

It melds and
blinds and
pushes through
to touch the towers and the money
and the hollow heart
(on what hallowed ground)
and teach me beauty
and sorrow
and solitude
and freedom.

# Looking Through Windows

My,
what lovely things!
How quaint and absurd—
the twinkle of vending machines,
the spooning of chairs,
the slick shine of the tables and
gum-speckled floors,
complacent and poised
beyond thin sheets of glass—
pretty rooms illuminated.
Little secrets, dioramic.
We all live in dollhouses.

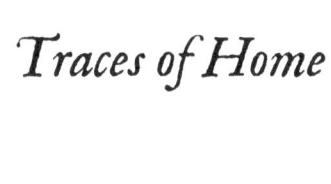

# Christmas Eve

Each of us is wrapped in light,
especially the children, glowing
with the aura of impatience.
Clove, orange, and rum glide on air.

The indoor chorus builds with each
stomp on the threshold, each coat
on the pile, each step into silver
and gold and Nat King Cole.

Sneaking from the front door
into the night's showering lace,
wearing my mother's boots and my
father's scarf, spirit inflating

in the blue-ice wind, a child can
wonder at such winter magic—
cyclones of crystal stirring in silence
over the pathways of the luminaries.

# July

If you could give months as gifts
I would wrap up July. I'd wrap it with Cool Whip
and sponge cake, firecrackers and diaphanous bugs,
and I would leave it on your doorstep.
You could open it when you got cold.
It could fill up your living room
and pour from the windows and
while everyone else had ten feet of snow
you could picnic. You could
raise your face to the sun.

# The Fourth of July

It begins with gunmetal-blue smoke,
signal of plenty, foreteller of burns on our tongues
from corn grilled in its own green silks.
The sun dips down languorously slow, the voices of this family
rise into a pale sky—the last memory I have
of all of us together.

As darkness falls you screw your face up tight. Your small
hands—still puffed with infancy—clamp over your ears.
It was cruel to find this funny.
Why shouldn't we fear these dying stars
and the horrible crash they make when they go?
I should've known. I should've given you comfort.

Beneath the cosmic, stunning colors,
feeling self-important and dancing to their pretty magic,
all was bliss for me in these final days. But you—
you were right to cower. You were right
to close your eyes while we celebrated our light;
while we tensed in expectation.

## Summer Storm

The laden air is sweet.
Covered porches become grottos in the deluge.
Verdant whispers are punctuated by the brontide—
a deep, drowned sound
pounding further,
farther,
further,
farther
off.

Glacé atop the cobblestones,
reflected images dart—
sky praising branches
and hands
turn up.
Wings slip
through a slate sky
growing lavender
and bruised.

An ice cream truck moseys
at the far end of the lane,
turning onto Green Bay Road and
trailing a warped tune
which soaks
into the atmosphere and
fades
across
the
lake.

# Thanksgiving Firsts

Who will slip from the guest room first
this year—leave behind the sound of even breath
and triumphantly join silent Uncle Kevin in the kitchen
where the coffee sputters into a glass pot
and the newscasters mutter
incomprehensibly above the microwave?

Who will be the first to heap sugar
over expanses of crackling cereal, and skim it back
from the top like a sweet, melting snow?
Or the first to finish dressing in velvet and
patent leather, and run into the skeletal woods
behind the house?

Finally, side-by-side on the oriental rug,
tracing geometric flowers and beasts
and falling asleep to the banter—
*too much pumpkin pie, too many buttered rolls,*
*too many days so far apart from one another—*
who will be the first to go?

# The Snow Makes Me Think of Death

The snow makes me think of death.
Once pure—a blameless material for houses,
harmless weapons, clean slates, sled slopes,
men with dark smiles and twiggy arms held wide
to the big, beautiful world—
it's different now.

It makes me think of the boy
who wrapped his hands around my waist
when we were fourteen.
I recall a friend rushing to warn me—
he was looking for *me*
in that dark, crowded, colorful gymnasium.

Never having danced
beyond a ring of lip-glossed girls
in glitter-coated camisoles, I was afraid.
If I accepted his invitation, was I inviting
something more?

I made my way to the double doors while
Boyz II Men played over the speakers.
Hesitating at the threshold I told myself to
*Stay. Don't be unkind.*
That was when he tapped me on the shoulder.

I remember thinking that his hands were huge—
that they could cover both sides of me entirely.
I rested my palms high up on his shoulders, glancing at him
once or twice. He had grown into his hairy arms
that had seemed so grossly manly in the second grade.

On the last day before summer I told him
I would like us to be *friends*.

We didn't talk much after that.
Truth be told, we hadn't talked much *before*.
He wrote, "Stay real"
on the back page of my yearbook.

One weekend in December,
amusing ourselves in the alleyway behind our house,
my sister and I struggled to upturn a garbage can
which had filled to the brim with dense, wet, snow.
He came striding down the narrow lane from his home
a few garages down and smiled at us.

I was conscious of him
and his smile
and mild manner.
I was conscious of my hair—
curled wildly from the impact
of the flurries.

In a few smooth and simple gestures
he took hold of the can, put it on its head, and shook.
How we cheered when that revolting mold emerged—
half white, half pink with refuse.
He chuckled and he walked back home.

Thirteen years later, flying somewhere
through a dark December sky, I read the news—
it seemed the big, beautiful world
was not the right one for him,
and he had quietly taken his leave.

In a flood I thought of his hands over my waist,
the snow falling slowly, the wild curls I couldn't hide,
his squinted, smiling eyes
before he walked away,
his gift of a dance—my first—

in a time when no one looked twice at me.

I think of the snow falling
when he upended these things.
And that is why now,
the snow
only makes me think of death.

# Homesick

Chicago spurs
a pool of lights—
cheering,
viscous, stellar, bright motion
without pause.

Deep within the suburbs
all that's seen from emerald squares
of lawn: a tangerine haze staining a
dark, mulberry night. No outliers, only
major constellations here.

For better or worse
these half-stars and manicured yards
are my comfort and my ruin.
The things I long for.
The things that repulse.

# Threads

When I came home
I traced my threads
to a blue house (or was it gray?).
I see it in the fabric
of my dreams
to this day.

# Beasts of Wilmette

A paste of dirt and rainwater
smeared on smooth cheeks.
Cakes of muck in our hands.
Clover stems woven flat are pressed between palms
and hurled into the air while their tiny little heads
lay tucked behind our ears.

Birch and oak and maple wave over our wildling rituals.
The skull of an acorn cracked; innards spat out
are ground with heels back into the earth.
Milkweeds lure the butterflies to feast and the cattails
on the dunes hail high, thin white clouds
streaking over the blue-green waves.

How we love the world to be clawed up
by our fingernails and stuck there—
twenty dark-realm crescent moons.
How we love to tear the bark as we climb and
pluck the golden tops of weeds and smear them
across our inner forearms, to stain.

Wild, loose, unstoppable.
How I miss this now that the days are long and
I'm so prim and cleanly—
so utterly tame and exhausted—
now that everything and everyone
has its place.

# War

Around the field of mongrels
    I found a piece of twine
And held it up unto the sun
    To find that it was mine.

Disintegrating piece of string
    Decaying, fraying line
Plucked from 'neath the mud and stone
    Amongst the blood and grime.

Then I recalled at once a knot
    I'd tied when I was small
Long ago when veins were one—
    Amassed heart of us all.

Such accidental crimes that stole
    A knot that kept a truce!
Instead my well-meant speck of twine
    Became part of a noose.

And all of this before the war
    Between the flying chairs,
Before I threw the one at you
    And left you on the stairs.

Retreat! Retreat! It's not a choice
    We all must reconcile.
To sweep, to trim, to prune, to shine
    The devastating miles.

Now I kneel to dig a grave
    Where several feet below,
I lay the twine and grow a rope
    To climb out in the snow.

# On Leaving My House for the Last Time

I felt the plane departing from the house,
ripping up the floorboards as it went,
pulling at the railing on the stair,
bringing down the walls and windows
slowly.

I felt a shudder as it tore the roof
and felt the thudding down the front stone steps.
The wings shredded the kitchen cabinets
whose flowery knobs chimed sweet against the ground,
all else was silent.

The granite counter broke apart and crumbled.
The tail took down the ceiling; dust came raining to the floor
and filled the empty corners by the fireplace
where I once played and hid
when I was small.

The plane departed quietly from within
and left me standing speechless in the East
when I looked back and realized all was lost
and not for me to tidy
or make neat.

My hands are barred from touching those white doors,
I can no longer speak to any room
and rest my palm against the house's heart
when surely there I dwelt
not long ago.

From above the landscape all looked bruised—
an apple rotting in the autumn sun.
The closer to the ground I came I witnessed—
the trees on fire,

every single one.

# Shrapnel

Ask me for advice when you know better.
Ask me if it's time for you to leave and I won't say.
Wait six years and see if I have answers.
Wait six years and find that I have chewed off both my hands.

Sometimes memory rises from the blackout.
Sometimes I remember all the unintended shots—
missteps, questions, doubts—each taking something from me.
Breaking something in me. Giving something to me.

Pick. Pick. Pick. Pick. Pick the shards beneath.
Itch the skin and graze with teeth and break it all I say.
(Attempts at fast removing this thing buried deep within—
I get the feeling I might detonate.) And yet,

loving us is all that I know how or care to do.
Sometimes I find that loving means
to drink down shrapnel in a glass of booze.
Don't you fucking offer me another.

## Goodbye House

In a great blue house
There were frosted lamps
And humming black vents
And pictures of—

Four bright smiles on a tropical beach
And three ladies fair, sitting on chairs
And two little dogs and some pretty door knobs
And a ceiling paint chip and a gray basement
And a brush and pink phone and a yard full of bones
And a ghost in the night who turns on the lights
Goodbye house
Goodbye beach
Goodbye smiles on a tropical beach
Goodbye frosted lamps and humming black vents
Goodbye ladies fair, goodbye chairs
Goodbye dogs and
Goodbye knobs
Goodbye things and goodbye rings
Goodbye stone lane,
Goodbye blame
Goodbye paint chip and gray basement
Goodbye everything
Goodbye bones
Goodbye to the fright who turns on the lights
Goodbye oppressive, doleful air
Hello houses here and there.

*Based on the children's book "Goodnight Moon"*
*by Margaret Wise Brown*

# New Rooms

She smiled all day
And laughed with her mother
Toasted with wine
And said, "I'll have another."

She smiled all day
And said, "This is fine"
In the still of new rooms
With their new-floorboard shine

And when she returned
She sat on the toilet
Her face in her hands
And she wept.

# Scars

Vivid, star-like clustering over
my expansive body
of hope—you are my scars.
You are sides of the moon,
both the light
and the dark.
The cool rays of your impact
in radial spikes over my world.

Each of our Panglossian winters and
halcyon summers alight in my heart
and just like the moon to the tide
they pull me toward you,
propel me away.

I feel you and see you
wherever I am, wherever I go. My business—
to be your keeper forever. Let the night burn.
I turn to the daybreak
finding the blow of lost dreams,
and the burnished provenance
of a new one.

# A Different State

Recalling the pulsate drone
of cicada song in summertime,
I can nearly feel their shells
crunching underfoot in lush patches of grass
and with closed eyes, easily conjure that purple sky
tinged intrusively with light.

Each backyard hemmed in tall fences,
every front door spotlit and open, it was a
strange place and stranger time.
It was a different state—
loved deeply, mourned,
despised.

Out here the caterpillars in the wild woods
shick like scissors as they feast.
Frogs peep like birds within the tangled roots
in the densest gloom. Here, a star can bathe itself
in other stars and a road can wander.
I have arrived, and what a wonder.

# Reflection

I stand on the welcome mat
at the front door
of my childhood home
trying to see through the glass;
a shadow figure blocks my view.
I just want to know if they've
kept the carpet on the stairs,
if my name is still carved
in the sill of my bedroom window,
if they papered over the walls I painted
for my mother,
if I matter to this place
anymore,
or if it matters anymore
to me.

# The Architecture of Memory

I dreamt I was terrible
to my sister—cruel,
needlessly, and every demon
I ever deserved chased me from each
nook and cranny, each
hiding space.

My last chance in racing
to the basement, I paused on the landing.
Is that carpet, beneath my feet?
Is the wall flush, to my right?
Wasn't there an exit here?
Wasn't there another door?

Wasn't there another door?
Wasn't there another door?
Wasn't there another door?
Wasn't there another door?
Wasn't there another door?

## Who Are You, House?

We brush our teeth at the top of the stairs.
He inspects the texture of the walls
while I pick at a speck of paint discovered on the bannister.

We listen to the ceiling fans whirl
as we nod off to sleep, and in the morning heat
we listen to their tepid breeze again, each spin a whisper.

We send smoke and oil leaping from our pans,
the scent of bacon fills each room like a presence.
We learn the hardwood floor creaks everywhere.

We descend the stairs at an angle, as they are steep and
narrow. The light and shadows fall in unfamiliar shapes.
We make new ones ourselves. Nice to meet you, house.

*You I Have Loved*

# A Ghost I Knew

Sitting on a stone bench riddled with stains,
a summer evening in the city cools with night.
That I would drink of this air and still the hot sadness
of your forgetting.

I could see it coming on—
an unlocking of the eyes,
a hand released, a caress over your chest—
cold and still like the stone beneath.

It was a vanished passion you unleashed on me
in the soft, dark, nothing of last night.
Suddenly, we were three—you, a ghost I knew,
and me.

I saw him—thin, fair, faint above your bed—
when with a testing touch
you lay unfeeling and I knew
I was alone with him.

The loss doubles me over.
My weight now double-made
heaves with each
progressive step.

And yet, looking at your face I think I see
he who was familiar. I
will blame nothing
but myself.

## The Heart is a House

If I am a daisy,
   You are a rose.
If I am a letter,
   Then you are prose.
If I am a touch,
   Then you're an embrace.
If I am cotton
   You surely are lace.

If the heart is a house,
   Then you are within,
And we are of dust
   And smoke and skin,
Of sweetness and skies
   Of glimmering pools,
Of bonework and water,
   Your straight hair,
My curls.

Oh blue! Oh green!
   Oh aquamarine!
And free, fleet and fun
   I can run,
I can scream!
   And never once wish
To be more than I,
   For you are the roof
Of the house of my life.

# Daybreak

In the early morning
before the sun inches above our pretty little sliver of the sea,
you find me in the dark and drape me in your heady warmth.

Heartbeat to heartbeat, each murmuring
hypnotic words of love we can only understand
as a thrumming in our skin and bones.

This is language beyond language;
a meter more powerful than ours where two souls marry
and speak in time.

The whole world is awash beyond our safe nest.
When you hold me, all is light and all surrounding
blurs and bleeds together like an artwork left out in a summer rain.

You are the other piece of me—
I cannot distinguish where I end and you begin
and I have no desire to find the boundary.

Each day a new honeyed happiness,
a new glorious, citric sunrise. Never, never fading.
Always there is more, there is plenty.

In every dawning you bring with you my joy
and drive away distresses with your calm, patient,
firm and faithful self.

I want nothing when I hear your laugh, and look upon
your cheek caressed by your lashes. I want nothing
when we kiss, your breath wedded with mine.

I want nothing when you touch my skin, and fill the room
and all of me and all my world with your being.
Darling, you are it.

# Passersby

How I love to lay here
and to watch the hours with you—
while them all away
by simply letting them pass through.

The light will dance in leafy shadow
bounding in a pool,
but we will lay and watch and breathe
with little else to do.

The breeze may briskly enter
and the lanterns rattle there,
the neighbors pound with heavy foot
above and down the stair,

but I should rather lay here
with my fingers in your hair
and watch the bee that slips in
and retreats without a care.

The dog may bark and groan and huff
as she lays bored and still,
the cactus may turn brown and dry
forgotten on the sill.

The clock will skip upon a glance
and we will have our fill
of all the lazy hours
that two motionless can kill.

Oh how I love to lay here
and to watch the minutes pass.
Let them go without us,
let them hurry toward the past.

Forget the world and listen to it all,
so loud, so fast—
we don't need to speak, don't need the sound,
don't need the clash.

My hand upon your hand,
my heart beside your heart,
how fine it is to lose a day
not moving 'til the dark,

but I feel it has found us
as we slowed and heard it lark—
so lay with me my love
and let us watch the time depart.

## Joya

If I close my eyes I can see her still—
pink slippers on her feet, floral-print nightgown,
amber curls, gray at the base, and hands shaped like
momma's, stirring Lipton soup on the electric stove.

Throats closing in the afterglow of
innumerable packs of her cigarettes,
we'd humbly accept two bowls of steaming neon broth
and sip down every last "o" in the bowl,

which reminds me—her love was so great
that her mouth would make such a shape
as she stretched out the words,
"Oh it's so good to see you!"

# Her Hands
*(A poem by my mother, Nancy T. Schonberg)*

Bent and twisted.
Scarred and scored by too many things
not remembered.
Nails tapered, softly painted.
Old with curly networks of veins.
Untold hours upon years into decades of work.
Cooking, cleaning, ironing. Loving.
What was yours and what wasn't.
Sold.
Free.
Strong hands never failed.
Soft, soothing ever and always.
Swift with discipline.
Later tap, tapping your pain.
Always present.
No words of complaint only tapping with
Those hands I love and live in awe of.
Their quiet, important presence no longer here.
Always here.

8/29/2009

## Corta Pero Ancha

How many times can you dine out
or pull on a sweater fresh from the dryer
or hear that favorite song
or watch the sun sink low
or smell the rain, the petrichor,
or walk the path to your doorway,
turn the last page, or gaze upon the sea before
it isn't all that special anymore? Any of it?
I wonder if this day exists and if
it finds us all, eventually.

Some days may be destined
to be unremarkable but some
begin in glory.
Soft and gentle, the loosening of stars and
the radiating of color:
emerald green, a melt of pale jade,
peach, rose, and lilac—
each emerging before grand crescendos
in electric tangerine. And softly, placidly
(with pomp), butter and gold.

*La vida es corta pero ancha*
my grandfather said,
and in his eyes I saw his youth, racing.
I saw his spirit, blazing.
I think he was telling me that
there is always more passion—
there is always passion for more.
The road will not be long for us
and for this, in part, I think I'm grateful—
I will have enough. It will be
beautiful. It will be full.

It will be wide.

## Mainly in the World

I miss you each
and every
day,
but spotted somehow
in the flashing leaves and
aloft upon the arias
of birds and
in the sun
itself—
there you are.
Sometimes even
in the mirror, but
mainly in the
world.

# Benediction

I went to the cemetery today.
Followed the long, hooked drive
to a sea of stone soldiers
and rippling flags.

I stopped being afraid of walking over graves
when I found one I was looking for—
when I found someone
I loved.

It felt good to dig—to be in touch—
to rend and rip the weeds
and free a stone's periphery.
To sweep the dirt from a name.

I left with soil beneath my fingernails
and smeared across my forehead
like ashes from church—
warm, soft, and light.

## It Helps, a Little

A cup of tea won't
fill the inner void but
it helps, a little.
Lighting a candle will not
cure a sickened heart,
but it helps,
a little.
A strong embrace won't
mend what's broken or
bring back
what's lost,
but,
it helps a little.

# How to Turn on a Lamp

There on the table in the hall, reach beneath the bell
of the shade and grabble in the dark below the harp
until at last your fingers grasp the knob, high on the neck.
With a twist, this adapted little sun
emerging from the socket will
illume.

In that instant and that instant only,
you might see your ghosts—
sitting in the armchair, sipping tea by the window,
standing at the bookshelf, looking upon you
with the glow of love.

## King Biko

Noble king crosses
his arms as he lays
splayed out on his belly.

Powdered poof on his head,
white beard on his chin,
dark eyes see little but

he walks proudly, even though he
limps with age and wears
ownership around his neck.

He grows senile and begs.
Royals should not beg but command
as he used to

for the scraps of my plate.
They are not worthy enough for him.
He would rather the stuff of his

bowels and the bones
of the ground with the taste
of the bitter green grass.

Noble king is mighty
and has become amiable albeit
slightly distasteful in his age.

I fear his death and love
his blue-gray curls all
the more with every day.

Beloved Biko—
in all your majesty and your

slow decline,
you old canine.

## Pocket-concert

I was four fingers deep in bourbon when I hit the floor,
laughing so hard that tears streamed from my eyes.
You were filming and I, woman who loves to put on a show,
couldn't choke out a word.
You and your pocket-concert—
phone blaring from the depth of your sweatpants—
are the funniest fucking thing in tie-dye and pigtails.
We two grown-ass women snickering on the kitchen tiles,
two spastic kids goading each other on, have a lot
to laugh and cry about.
I appreciate the idea that even if life is a bitch,
she is a bitch worth dancing with.

# Homecomings
*(A poem by my sister, Jesi P. Schonberg)*

Are all my feelings cyclical?
Am I at the age where I've felt every emotion already?
Happiness, hatred, sadness, love,
love.
Love.
And love.
Every time I've fallen in it, the feeling weakens.
Like I already know it, like love is the only home that
makes sense to me so coming back to it just feels like
walking in the front door and dropping your bags.
Maybe the people never mattered.
I know it mattered the first time.
When it was over,
the pain.
Shit... the pain.
The pain.
Every time I've fallen in it, the feeling weakens.
Like I already know it, like pain is the only home that
makes sense to me so coming back to it just feels like
walking in the front door and dropping your bags.
Maybe the people never mattered.
I know I matter.
Are all my feelings cyclical?

2/22/19

## Love Them Well

There was a time when I bared my fangs like a feral animal
because I loved them and still they fell away from me
like teeth from a child's mouth—
a death of a kind.

In view of life's repeated teachings and
the anesthetic of the years,
I'm simply grateful for our season.
It was only natural, like fire on a log,
beads of rain from a cloud,
winds across the sea touching a sail—
you in my life.

In part I learned no family is forever
and no friend a guarantee, and yet,
present in any togetherness I know now, I see—
love them well.
Delight in them, fiercely.
Forgive them already.
Forgive yourself.

# In Here

We dream of a home
and how to fill it,
and how its heart will beat
each time we take the stair.
We see it so clearly—
a window is always open.
In the dusk, locusts hum,
lamplight is yellow, thick.
Leaves inhale day and exhale night.
The clean air breezing
through the screen door
will cool our brows.
There will be kind words
and hot dinners on our plates
and a sacerdotal dog
beneath the table, frowning.
There will be laughing.
There will be lazy twilight
and sparrows darting
like love and music do
in here.

## Home is the Heart

When the broad walkway has been blown clear of small leaves,
and the smooth pale stone is mottled by a filtered light,
I have found my home.

When the museum face is polished by the early morning sun,
and within, the echoes of a thousand voices carrying the heavy,
love-drenched threads of Art leak out to drench my feet and
the mottled walkway, I have found my home.

When the breeze is soft and the windows glint;
when the sky is pale blue like a cornflower and the air
smells of sweet grass; when I recognize no one and remember
myself, I have found my home.

Home isn't where the heart is.
Home is the heart.

# Acknowledgements

Special thanks and great love to mom and dad
who taught me how to explore this world with wonder
and who gave me the tools to do it, too.

With eternal love and appreciation for my late grandfather,
Kenneth Carlos Schonberg, who by now has surely made
1,001 friends in the hereafter. Kindred spirit—
you are the submerged pearl in the ocean of my love.
I strive to make you proud.

*La vida es corta pero ancha*
*-Excelsior-*

# Indexes

# Index by Title

Alluvia - 46
The Architecture of Memory - 109
Autumnal - 28

Beasts of Wilmette - 99
Behind You - 36
Benediction - 123
Bones - 55
Breath - 17
On Burning Bridges - 54
But Then it Aches - 60

Christmas Eve - 89
Cloud - 25
Corta Pero Ancha - 120

Daybreak - 115
A Different State - 107
Directions - 63
Dislocation - 58
Down by the Water - 67

The Egret - 30

Fear Names - 70
First Sights - 20
The Fly - 29
For a Friend - 40
The Fourth of July - 91

Garden Dream - 22
Gazing at the Chapel - 81

A Ghost I Knew - 113
Goodbye House - 104
Gravestones - 74

He's Not That Into You - 39
The Heart is a House - 114
Her Hands (By NTS) - 119
Home is the Heart - 132
Homecomings (By JPS) - 129
Homesick - 97
Hopping Over Garden Walls - 24
How to Turn on a Lamp - 125

Ice - 19
In Here - 131
Intravenous - 59
It Helps, a Little - 124

J.L.C. - 37
Joya - 118
July - 90

King Biko - 126

On Leaving My House for the Last Time - 101
Limbo - 73
Looking Through Windows - 86
Losing Pieces - 57
Love Them Well - 130

Mainly in the World - 122
Mimes - 83
Mt. Desert Island - 41
My Friend David - 75

New Boston - 85

New Rooms - 105

Often He is Dreaming - 32
Often I am Dreaming - 15
On Guard - 26
The Owl - 76

Passersby - 116
Phantom Hollow - 72
Pocket-concert - 128

The Raven - 77
Reflection - 108
Refugees - 47
Return from Vacation - 42
Reveries - 31

Scars - 106
Sea Stone - 73
Shock and Stifle - 56
Shrapnel - 103
The Snow Makes Me Think of Death - 94
Somewhere a Train - 45
Springtime in Davis Square - 18
Star Fishing - 68
Steel - 82
Summer Storm - 92
Symphonies and Silence - 27
Synapses - 53

A Thought - 48
Thanksgiving Firsts - 93
Threads - 98

Wake-Up Call - 35
War - 100

We Are Conveyed - 49
Weekdays, 8:45 AM - 62
When - 61
Who Are You, House? - 110
Windblown Light - 16
Wording - 21
The Worship Game - 84

# Index by First Lines

*"All rise" a voice commands* - 49
*A cup of tea won't/fill the inner void but/it helps, a little* - 124
*A dollop of sun, pink /spill on window frost* - 19
*A loose lampshade sways like a church bell* - 41
*A man with a heart full of spiders and sorrow* - 72
*A nickel pressed in concrete* - 85
*A paste of dirt and rainwater/smeared on smooth cheeks* - 99
*A thin elastic cloud, /dull, gray morning light filling the room* - 20
*Are all my feelings cyclical?* - 129
*Around the field of mongrels/I found a piece of twine* - 100
*Ask me for advice when you know better* - 103
*At night I bring my fishing pole into the open plain* - 68
*At the root of all things is a heart* - 73

*Bent and twisted. /Scarred and scored by too many things* - 119

*Chicago spurs/a pool of lights* - 97
*Concrete sprouts/in heavy stems still rising/toward the sun* - 83

*Doesn't it feel like the walls of the world* - 28
*Down by the water/are two sequin skies* - 67

*Each of us is wrapped in light* - 89

*Heavenly pools manifest across the marshes* - 27
*Hopping over garden walls/I often feel the thorns* - 24

*How I love to lay here/and to watch the hours with you* - 116
*How many times can you dine out* - 120
*Hummingbird mind/flits over memory* - 31

*I don't know what lilac smells like* - 21
*I dreamt I was terrible/to my sister—cruel* - 109
*I felt the plane departing from the house* - 101
*I found it on the windowsill, /Waiting just for me* - 75
*I had a dream the other night/about a garden old and wild* - 22
*I miss you each/and every/day* - 122
*I stand on the welcome mat* - 108
*I thought I'd lost/my self* - 58
*I was four fingers deep in bourbon when I hit the floor* - 128
*I watched an egret soar/over the waters of the Charles* - 30
*I went to the cemetery today* - 123
*If I am a daisy, /You are a rose* - 114
*If I close my eyes I can see her still* - 118
*If you could give months like gifts/I would wrap up July.* - 90
*In a great blue house/There were frosted lamps* - 104
*In me, moving, wired, untamed* - 53
*In the early morning* - 115
*Inside is hot and roiling—/a pot ready to drain/and scald* - 59
*It begins with gunmetal-blue smoke* - 91

*Lacing fingers together en revés* - 84
*Landscapes of steel/took down our red bricks* - 82
*Let me hold onto this glinting revelation* - 25
*Like a hooped skirt/like a trellis* - 55

*Moored boats point in the direction of the wind* - 63
*My, /what lovely things!* - 86

*Name your fear something like "Henry,"* - 70
*Noble king crosses his arms as he lays splayed out* - 126

*Often he is dreaming/of the provenance of horses* - 32
*Often I am dreaming of the provenance of thrushes* - 15
*Once upon a time there was a girl with crimson curls* - 76

*Recalling the pulsate drone/of cicada song in summertime* - 107
*Red desert sands surround green scrub across the valley* - 46

*She lost her diamond ring/left it on a speckled countertop* - 57
*She smiled all day/And laughed with her mother* - 105
*Sitting on a stone bench riddled with stains* - 113
*Slow intestinal burns and/cardiac microsplosions* - 62
*Sometimes you think you've burned a bridge* - 54
*Sometimes you're glad to see/a bit of your own blood* - 60

*The air so still/I thought I could feel the lilies* - 42
*The fly between the window panes/Upon the windowsill* - 29
*The judgment of the wind/over the wheat proclaimed* - 45
*The laden air is sweet* - 92
*The petals fall, /silent, pale like/snow* - 18
*The photograph of us* - 36
*The propellers of a Saab 340b* - 48
*The shadows lie long and thick/in the parlor* - 26

*The smooth, sunbaked stone radiated heat in my closed fist* - 71
*The snow makes me think of death* - 94
*The things I've seen/fly wingless* - 17
*The urgency of night knows* - 39
*The years collect on once gleaming surfaces* - 47
*There lived a woman in a tower/Made of shining ivory stone* - 77
*There on the table in the hall, reach beneath the bell* - 125
*There was a time when I bared my fangs* - 130
*There's a windblown light/Coming in through my window* - 16
*Tonight tight constellations/spin out high over the steeples* - 81

*Upon the pretty flower beds* - 74

*Vivid, star-like clustering over/my expansive body/of hope* - 106

*Waiting for the light/at the broad intersection* - 37
*We brush our teeth at the top of the stairs* - 110
*We dream of our home* - 131
*We ride into the night across a river of asphalt and dust* - 40
*When I came home/I traced my threads* - 98
*When stars reappear for me/and the catch in my chest* - 61
*When the broad walkway has been blown clear* - 132
*Who will slip from the guest room first/this year* - 93
*With the fan pondering east and west* - 35

*You can button up/from sternum to throat* - 56

# Index by Date

❁

*Most of these poems have seen countless iterations over the years. If I were to date them by the time they were last edited or amended, many of them would be dated 2019, and that just wouldn't feel right. Instead, I dated them by their "birthdays," if you will, in order to honor when they first came me. If a poem is entirely (or mostly) unchanged from its original format, it will be noted with "*"*

## 2002

*The Fly** - 29

## 2004

*Star Fishing [October 19]** - 68

## 2005

*King Biko [November 13]** - 126
*Sea Stone [May 20]** - 71

## 2006

*First Sights* - 20
*Windblown Light\** - 16

## 2008

*Gravestones [November 11]\** - 74
*July [July 15]* - 90
*Somewhere a Train [April 27]\** - 45

## 2009

*Behind You [July 14]\** - 36
*Goodbye House [October 10]\** - 104
*Homesick* - 97
*J.L.C. [September 26]\** - 37
*On Leaving My House for the Last Time [October 13]\** - 101
*Limbo [March 13]\** - 73
*New Rooms [October 10]\** - 105
*Reflection* - 108
*Shrapnel [November 1]* - 103
*Summer Storm [May 6]* - 92
*Wake-Up Call [August 6]* - 35
*War [November 14]\** - 100

## 2010

*A Thought* [*March* 25]\* - 48
*Bones* [*March* 4] - 55
*Christmas Eve* [*November* 1] - 89
*Cloud* [*November* 1st]\* - 25
*For a Friend* [*March* 25] - 40
*Gazing at the Chapel* [*March* 4]\* - 81
*He's Not That Into You* [*November* 6th] - 39
*Ice* [*January* 29]\* - 19
*Looking Through Windows* [*March* 5]\* - 86
*Mimes* [*March* 5]\* - 83
*Mt. Desert Island* [*October* 31] - 41
*The Owl* [*October* 21]\* - 76
*Phantom Hollow* [*July* 27]\* - 72
*Refugees* [*January* 31] - 47
*Return from Vacation* [*October* 31] - 42
*Steel* [*March* 4] - 82
*We Are Conveyed* [*March* 25] - 49

## 2011

*A Ghost I Knew* - 113
*Down by the Water* [*December* 24] - 67
*Fear Names* [*June* 7]\* - 70
*Home is the Heart* [*August* 11] - 132
*New Boston* [*August* 22] - 85
*Scars* [*March* 16] - 106
*Springtime in Davis Square* [*February* 14] - 18

## 2012

*Garden Dream* [*January 9*] - 22
*The Heart is a House* [*January 10*]* - 114
*Threads* [*May 22*]* - 98

## 2013

*On Burning Bridges* [*August 14*]* - 54
*Dislocation* - 58

## 2014

*Passersby* [*January 12*] - 116
*Synapses* [*September 9*]* - 53

## 2015

*The Fourth of July* [*February 15th*] - 91
*Hopping Over Garden Walls* [*June 2nd*]* - 24
*Often He is Dreaming* [*April 8th*] - 32
*Often I am Dreaming* [*August 5th*] - 15

## 2017

*The Egret* - 30
*Intravenous [May 22]** - 59
*My Friend David** - 75
*The Raven** - 77
*Reveries* - 31
*When** - 61

## 2018

*A Different State [September]* - 107
*Alluvia* - 46
*The Architecture of Memory** - 109
*Autumnal [September 24]* - 28
*Beasts of Wilmette [February 21]* - 99
*Benediction* - 123
*Breath** - 17
*But Then it Aches [January 29]* - 60
*Corta Pero Ancha* - 120
*Daybreak [February 14]** - 115
*Directions* - 63
*Wording [October 9]* - 21
*How to Turn on a Lamp [September 30]* - 125
*It Helps, a Little** - 125
*Joya [September 29]** - 118
*Losing Pieces [September 28]* - 57
*Mainly in the World** - 122
*On Guard** - 26
*Pocket-concert [October 2]** - 128

*Shock and Stifle* - 56
*Symphonies and Silence* - 27
*Thanksgiving Firsts [September 27]* - 93
*Weekdays, 8:45 AM [November]* - 62
*Who Are You, House? [July]* - 110
*The Worship Game\** - 84

# 2019

*In Here [January 28]* - 131
*Love Them Well [January 19]\** - 130
*The Snow Makes Me Think of Death [February 13]\** - 94